I0018058

## Table of Contents

# Parts of a Computer

## Clock (2 GHz)

Controls speed of microprocessor. Advertised: 2GHz

(2,000,000,000 instructions per second)

## Hard Disk

Purpose: Permanent storage for programs and data files, that is, Windows, Word, Excel, Internet Explorer, pictures, songs, letters, reports, etc
Advertised: 500GB
500GB= 500,000,000,000 Byte locations

## Display

Gets bytes from memory for creating screen images

## Microprocessor

**Central piece of hardware.**
4 billion transistors
Purpose: execute program instructions
Advertised: Pentium or AMD

## Memory

RAM (Random Access Memory)
Purpose: Temporary Storage for Programs and data files. Programs must be transferred from the Hard Disk into memory in order to run
Advertised: 2GB (2,000,000,000) byte locations)
Very important to have at least 2GB for good performance

## Keyboard

Typing sends bytes to memory

## Modem

Converts bytes from memory into analog signals for communicating to the Internet

## Mouse

Sends signals to memory for communicating with the microprocessor

## Printer

Receives bytes from memory for printing characters and graphics

## CD-RW

Removable storage for programs, data files, pictures, songs. Referred to as a "burner" because of the laser beam recording.

## Flash Disk

Replacement for floppy disks. Removable storage for saving programs, data files, pictures, songs. Large electronic capacity, small size, rugged.

# The Physical Parts

This page gives added understanding to the discussion on How a Computer Works as described from a functional standpoint using the previous page "Parts of a Computer". The power supply, hard disk, floppy disk, and CD drive have been disassembled from the tower case so as to provide a relationship between the functional part and the physical part.

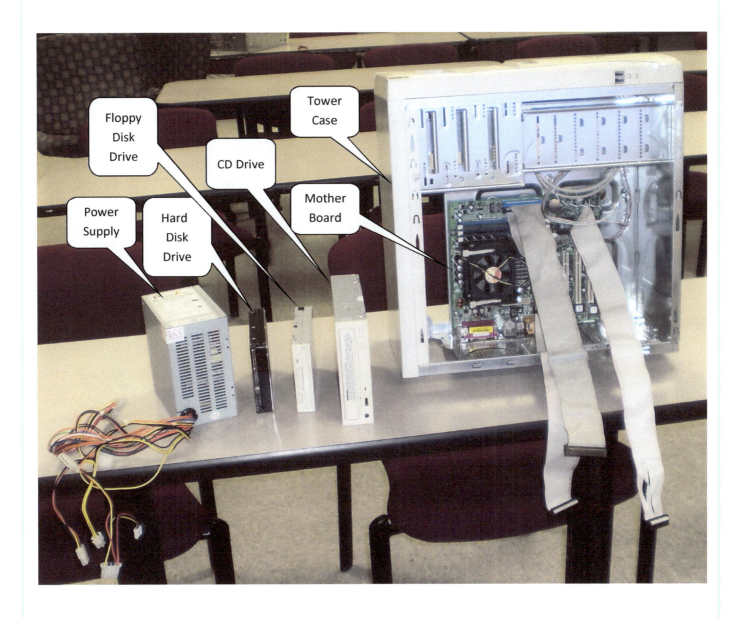

← Header

**OBSERVING SYSTEM PROPERTIES** ← Title

← Rationale

The System Properties window provides a quick method of determining basic information about your computer, such as the version of Windows, the level of Service Pack that has been downloaded by Microsoft, the type of microprocessor chip that is installed on the motherboard, the clock rate which is what drives the speed of the microprocessor, the number of cores within the processor, the installed memory, whether it is 32 bit or 64 bit system, and the name of the computer.

← Steps

Screen Shots

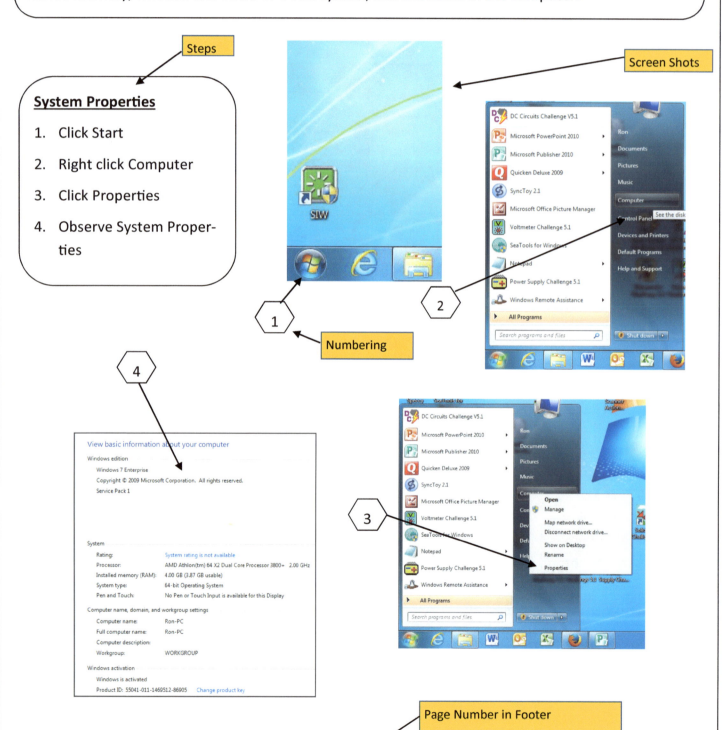

### System Properties

1. Click Start
2. Right click Computer
3. Click Properties
4. Observe System Properties

Numbering

# Hard Disk Usage

Most users of the computer have a false idea of what is being stored on their computer and where. In fact, the expression is often heard "my memory is getting full" when unbeknownst to them, it is really the hard disk getting full. For most of us, the amount of hard disk received at the time of purchase, is far more than ever needed. It is rare to find the used space over 50%. Therefore, this is a good tool to show the customer the amount of storage space still available for storing more programs, pictures, music, etc.

## Checking Hard Disk Usage

1. Double-click My Computer.
2. Right-click Local Disk (C:).
3. Click Properties.
4. Note the bytes of Used, Free, and Capacity.

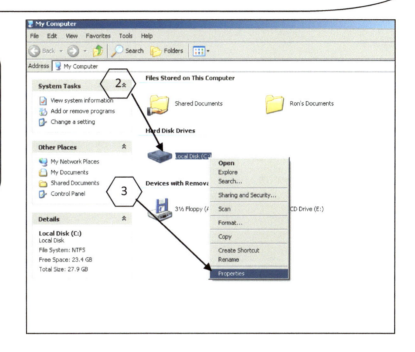

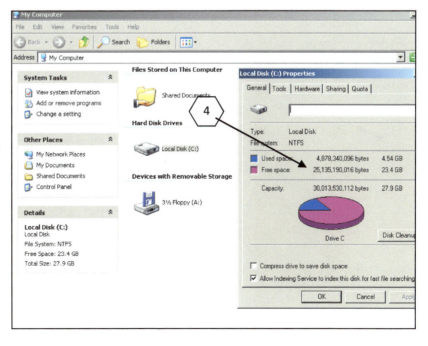

# Disk Cleanup

Disk Cleanup is a Windows maintenance utility that provides for the removing of unneeded files that have built up on your hard disk. Running this task frees up hard disk space and provides the potential for improving overall performance. Run this once per month and preferably prior to doing a defragment.

## Performing a Disk Cleanup

1. Open the Hard Disk Properties window.
2. Write down the 10 digit bytes of Used Space
3. Click the Disk Cleanup button
4. Observe the "calculating"
5. Check all of the items shown
6. Click OK, then Yes, and observe the progress of the cleaning.
7. When finished, check the used space for being a smaller number.

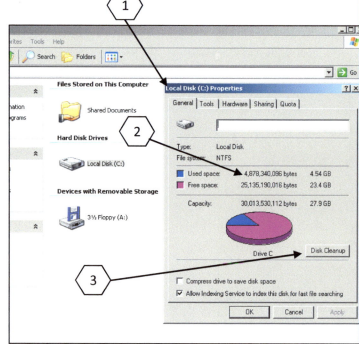

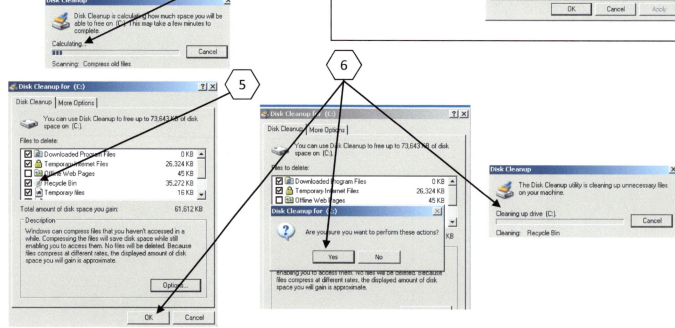

# Windows Check Disk

Check Disk (Chkdsk) checks the overall condition of the Hard Disk. Since the hard Disk is a mechanical device, it is more subject to failure than other parts of the computer. Check Disk checks for physical failure pertaining to the motors and read heads as well as software failure pertaining to corrupted files. Failure of either type, it attempts to correct. Run this at six month intervals or sooner should your computer be more than 2 years old.

## To Run the Check Disk Program

1. Perform the steps in "Hard Disk Usage" (pg.9) to get the Local Disk Properties window.
2. Click the Tools tab.
3. Click the Check Now button
4. Click check-marks into both Check Disk options.
5. Click Start
6. Note the message that Check Disk cannot run when Windows is running.
7. Click Yes and Restart your computer.
8. Check Disk will start running as the boot cycle starts back up.

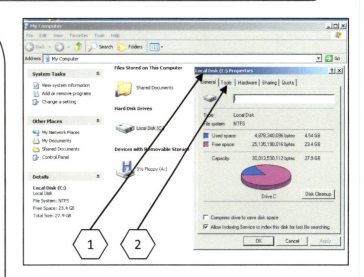

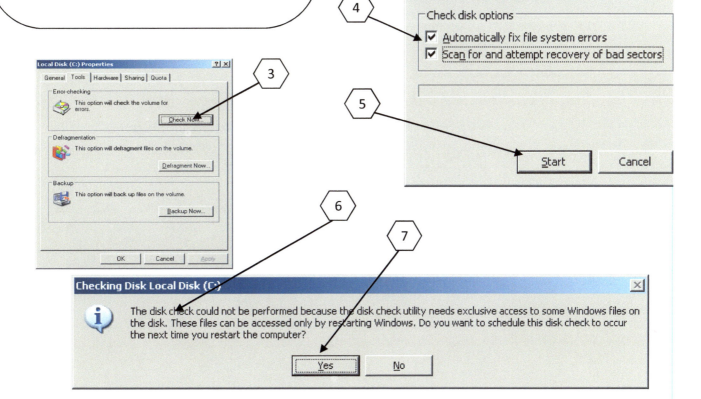

# Backing Up User Files

Backing up your user files is a very important part of maintaining your computer.  This means letters that you have written, spreadsheets, databases, pictures from your camera, music that you have downloaded, income tax files, personal finance files, etc. Backing up means to save a copy of the contents to a removable device such as a external Hard Disk (recommend an 200GB size) or a Flash Disk (recommend an 32GB size). Then store the removable device in a safe place so as to prevent it from being stolen or damaged.

### Procedure for Backing Up User Files Windows Vista & Windows 7

1.  Insert your backup device (Flash Disk or External Hard Disk) into any USB port. USB ports  can be found on the front, side, or rear of your computer.

2.  From the Windows desktop, click the START button.

3.  Find your name in the upper right corner of the Start Menu.  Click it.

4.  Note that a "yourname" folder opens and displays all of your personal user files.

5.  Hold down the CTRL key and click the following folders: CONTACTS, DESKTOP, FAVORITES, LINKS, MY DOCUMENTS, MY MUSIC, MY PICTURES, MY VIDEOS. They should all be selected (highlighted).

6.  Let up on the CTRL key. Then right-click  anyone of the highlighted folders.

7.  Point to SEND TO and then click on the icon  for your flash disk. This causes all of the selected folders to be copied to your backup device.

8.  Using MY COMPUTER, open the backup device and verify that the copy took place.

9.  Make a folder on the backup device (right-click on white space, click New, then folder).

10.  Rename the folder (use right-click) to Backup MMDDYYYY where the M,D,Y are the current date.

11.  Drag all of the backed-up folders onto the Backup MMDDYYYY

12.  Most users have just the one account set up on their computer. However, if you have individual accounts for other users, then repeat steps 1-11 for all other accounts.

# Clearing Cache, Cookie, and History Files

## Clearing Cache, Cookies, History files

While browsing the Internet, your computer uses cache and history files to store specific information about a Web page on your hard drive. These files enable the browser to find the same pages more quickly when you access them later.

The cache file stores page information for quick retrieval; a cached page is accessed more easily than the original page; frequent updates by the browser ensure you are getting the most recent version.

The history file stores a running list of the sites you have visited in a given time period. Please remember each time you access a new page, new information is added to your hard drive that uses valuable space. Therefore, the cache and history files should be cleared on a regular basis--daily, if you visit a number of pages. Allowing information to accumulate in these files will slow your download speed.

If a web page is not displaying properly, or is displaying content that you believe is not current, the solution in most instances is to clear your Internet Explorer cache and cookie files.

## Clearing Cache, Cookies, History files

1. Open the Internet Explorer window.
2. Click Tools from the menu bar (note: if the Menu Bar is not showing, go to the right side of the open window, click Tools, click Menu Bar)
3. Click Internet Options.
4. Click Delete
5. Click the Delete Files, then the Delete Cookies, and finally, Delete History.

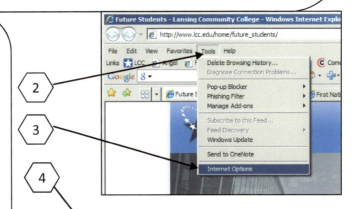

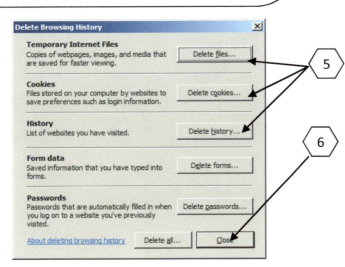

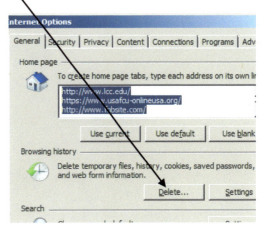

# Uninstalling Programs

There are many reasons why we may want to uninstall a program. One, it came installed from the factory and we just don't need it (games). Two, our current anti-virus program needs to be removed before we can install a recently purchased new one. Three, a webpage appeared indicating that our computer has problems and we made the mistake of allowing a "free scan" of our hard disk (Rogue Malware). Four, we downloaded a program from the Internet, tried it, and now want to remove it. CAUTION: Some of the installed programs listed are required for proper running of your computer. Be certain of what you are deleting.

### Uninstalling a Program

1. Click the Start button.

2. Click Control Panel

3. Click Programs, Uninstall a program. Note your computer may be set to bypass this step. If so, then click on Programs and features to get the screen as shown for step #4.

4. Right click the program to be uninstalled

5. Click UNINSTALL

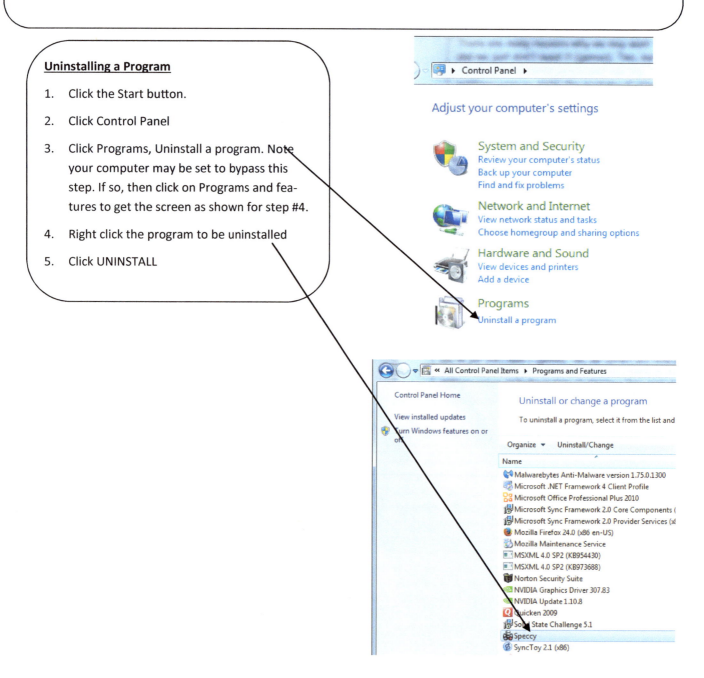

# Preventive Maintenance Daily & Weekly

## Daily:

1. Manage your email
   - Delete email from unknown sources
   - Do not open untrusted attachments
   - Organize into folders

## Weekly

1. Verify that anti-virus, anti-spyware, and firewall indicate "protected"
   - Open security icon on system tray
   - Subscription has not expired.
   - Virus definition files are being updated.
2. Scan the hard disk for malware
   - Use installed security software, Norton, McAfee, etc.
   - Schedule automatic scan
   - Use Malewarebytes Anti-Malware free download
   - Finds maleware with a different formula
   - Runs only when executed by the user
3. Check Windows Firewall in the Control Panel for an active firewall.
   - Firewall may be from Windows or from installed Internet Security package.
4. Run Windows Updates from the Start Menu
   - Initiate installation of outstanding important updates
5. Optimize performance
   - Run Disk Cleanup (see page 6)
   - Run Disk Defragmenter
   - Run Check Disk (see page 7)
   - Run Windows Defender to detect & eliminate spyware
6. Backup user files (see page 8)
7. Cleanup Web browser files (see page 9)

# Preventive Maintenance Monthly, Quarterly, Annually

## Monthly

1. Keyboard (brush keys, blow out with can of compressed air, soap and water on keys))
2. Liquid Crystal Display (For dry wipe, use microfiber cloth as used with cleaning eyeglasses. For screens a deeper cleaning, distilled water with 10% white vinegar)
3. Mouse, Roller ball type: remove bottom cover, scrape the dirt from the rollers with fingernail/Q-tip
4. Mouse, Optical Laser/Led-Photodiode type: wipe bottom with distilled water, change battery(s)
5. Clean grills (use household vacuum)
6. Check position (off the floor to reduce dirt/dust)
7. Check for adequate ventilation surrounding the system unit
8. Fans
9. Check the internal temperature using Speccy, should be less than 50C (122F)
10. Check the power strip for MOV working and good ground, see red and green LED indicators
11. Reseat easily accessible connectors
12. Uninstall unused user application programs (see page 10)
13. Check line speed (www.speakeasy.net)
14. Monitor system performance (CPU should idle at 0-4%)
15. ADVANCED EXPERTISE USER RECOMMENDED
    - Re-seat the power connector
    - Re-seat USB connectors
    - Remove unwanted programs (see page XX)
    - Eliminate unnecessary startup programs (see task manager, msconfig)
    - Clean inside the computer case

## Quarterly

ADVANCED EXPERTISE RECOMMENDED
- Vacuum first to remove as much dust as possible especially from the CPU heat sink being careful NOT to touch the motherboard electronics. Use special compressed air available at computer retail stores to rid the interior of remaining dust.

## Annual

ADVANCED EXPERTISE REQUIRED
- Clean install the Hard Disk, aka Full Recovery.
- Clean and apply fresh conductive paste to the microprocessor heat sink

# Malwarebytes Anti-Malware Scanner

Having a good Internet Security Package installed on your computer is the first defense in preventing virus and spyware. Norton, McAfee, and PC-Cillin are examples. However, Malwarebytes is another good choice for scanning your hard disk when you suspect a virus. It is a free download from the Internet that only runs when you tell it to do so. Therefore it does not run in competition with your installed anti-virus program. This program seems to find virus when others do not. I suggest uninstalling it when you have finished your scan otherwise you might be pestered to buy the full version.

## Downloading Malwarebytes

1. The following steps apply to using the Firefox browser.

2. Google "malwarebytes" using Firefox

3. Select the link pointing to malwarebytes.org

4. Click Free Download

5. Enter any email address, real or otherwise (bharris@yahoo.com should work)

6. Submit

7. Click SAVE. The setup file will be saved into your Downloads folder.

8. Click the Start Button (lower left corner)

9. Click yourname (upper right)

10. Double-click the Downloads folder.

11. Double-click the Malwarebytes setup (mbam-setup)

12. The installation of Malwarebytes begins.

13. Follow the prompts until complete.

14. Malwarebytes should automatically start but if not, go to the Programs menu and start it there.

15. Run a "Quick Scan" first.

16. Click remove to delete and quarantine.

17. Run and scan again to verify that the virus has been removed.

18. UNINSTALL Malwarebytes.

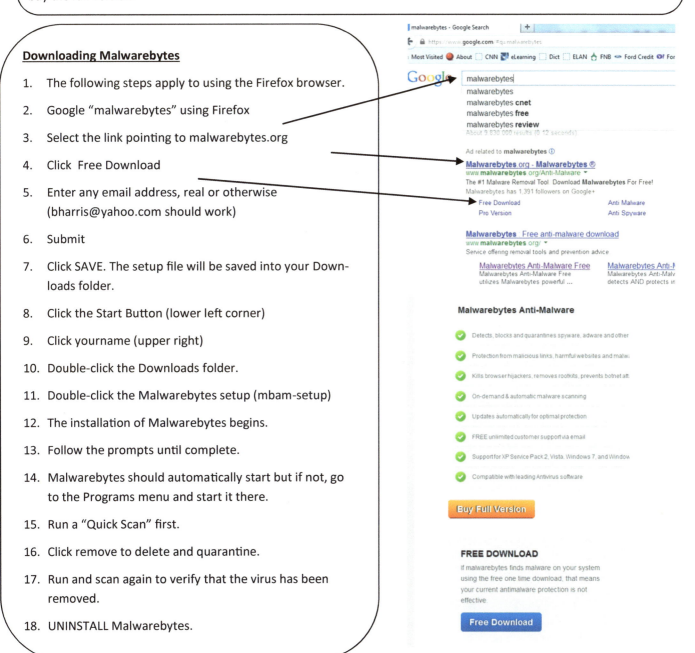

## Installing a New Hard Drive Using Recovery CDs Windows XP

<u>PURPOSE</u>: This procedure assumes that a hardware failure has occurred. When you attempt to boot, the display indicates "Operating System Not Found". You come to the first and most obvious conclusion that the Hard Drive has failed. Replacement is in order.

<u>PROCEDURE:</u>

1. Disconnect all peripheral cables except the mouse, keyboard, display, and Ethernet Lan cable.
2. Remove the bad Hard Drive.
3. Check the jumper configuration on the new drive to match that of the old drive. Install the new drive.
4. Power on and tap the F11 function key until the blue screen "Select First Boot Device" appears.
5. Insert the Windows XP Recovery CD into the CD drive. Arrow down to CD/DVD. Tap Enter. This forces the BIOS to select the CD drive as the first place to look for a bootable device. If a boot record is found on the CD, then the BIOS requests that you tap any keyboard key so as to confirm that it is truly your intention to read and therefore record (overwrite) data from the CD to the hard disk.
6. Windows Setup begins and loads files that it needs to erase the current content and then write a fresh copy of Windows XP.
7. From here the Setup will require several responses:
   - Tap Enter to Setup Windows XP now
   - Tap F8 to agree to the license agreement.
   - Tap ESC to install a fresh copy of Windows.
   - Tap ENTER to install on the C: partition.
   - Tab C confirming your choice in the previous step.
   - Arrow up/down and select Quick Format using the NTFS file system.
   - Tap F confirming your understanding that from this point on, all programs and user files will be erased.
8. Formatting begins which in the case of a Quick Format, erases only the File Allocation Table (FAT)
9. Windows files are then copied and written over the existing data.
10. Eventually an automatic reboot occurs which finds the Recovery CD still installed. The message "Tap Any Key to Boot from the CD" should be IGNORED. Instead allow the reading of additional installation files.
11. From here several responses are required:
    - NAME: customer name
    - Product Key: 25 digit usually found on the case
    - Administrator Password: leave blank
    - WORKGROUP computer
    - Connect through a LAN for Internet access

# SPECCY

**Speccy** is an advanced System Information tool for your PC. It basically tells you what is inside your computer. But more than that, it provides in-depth and detailed information which can be very helpful for the technician who may be attempting to diagnose and repair problems. See the screenshot below which shows the items addressed by the Speccy program. In addition, real-time temperatures within the CPU, Motherboard, and Hard Drive are also given.

Downloading the install file can be done from the Piriform website as shown below:

## http://www.piriform.com/speccy

# HD TUNE HARD DRIVE TESTER

HD Tune is a Hard Disk utility which scans the surface checking for errors and calculating performance by showing transfer rates and average access time.

## HD TUNE:

Go to www.hdtune.com.

Click on the HD Tune download link, ie the one that indicates "free for personal use".

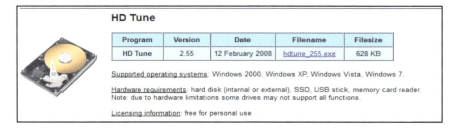

From your Downloads folder, double-click the install program **hdtune_255.exe** . Once installed, verify that HD Tune is listed within the Programs menu. Running the program should produce test results as shown below.

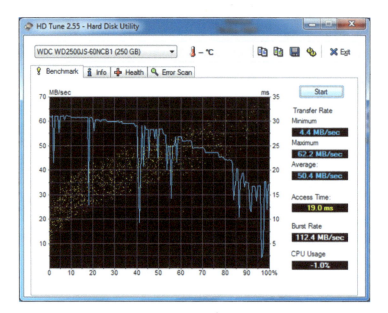

# DISK THRUPUT TESTER

**DiskTT** (Disk Throughput Tester) measures the performance of your harddrive`s read and write function. You can select a folder or drive to test and the program performs a real-time test on the selected disk. .

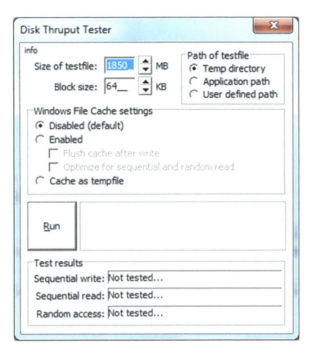

Downloading the install file can be done from the following web location:

**http://www.snapfiles.com/get/disktt.html**

# SUPER Pi CPU THRUPUT CHECKER

Super PI is a single threaded benchmark ideal for testing pure, single threaded x86 floating point performance and while most of the computing market has shifted towards multithreaded applications and more modern instruction sets, Super PI still remains quite indicative of CPU capability in specific applications such as computer gaming.

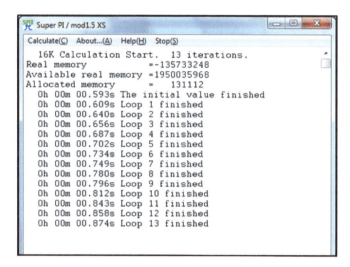

Downloading the install file can be done from the following web location:

**http://www.superpi.net/Download/**

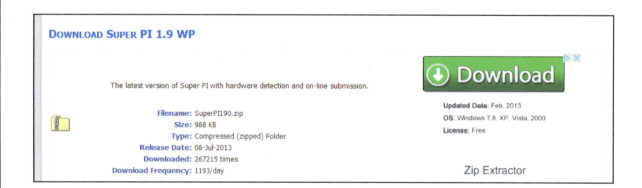

# MEMORY TEST

RAM sticks, known for their chip creep and random failures, are among the more annoying pieces of hardware to pinpoint as the source of a technical issue. Before you start digging around in the tower, it's best to start with a quick and free memory check via Windows. This way, you'll know whether or not it's worth swapping around sticks of RAM to see which one is the dud.

## MEMORY TEST

Step 1: Open the Start Menu and type in **mdsched.exe**, then press **enter**.

Step 2. A pop-up will appear on your screen, asking how you'd like to go about checking the memory. The first option will restart your machine and check the memory right now, and the second option checks the next time you choose to reboot. Pick the option that best suits your needs.

Step 3: Your computer will load a screen that shows the progress of the check and number of passes it will run on the memory. Watch the memory diagnostic tool for errors. If there are no errors, then it's likely that your RAM is not causing any issues, and it's time to investigate other hardware or software issues.

# PASSMARK BENCHMARK TEST

**PassMark PerformanceTest** ™ allows you to objectively benchmark a PC using a variety of different speed tests and compare the results to other computers.

Downloading the install file can be done from the following web location:

## https://www.passmark.com/products/pt.htm

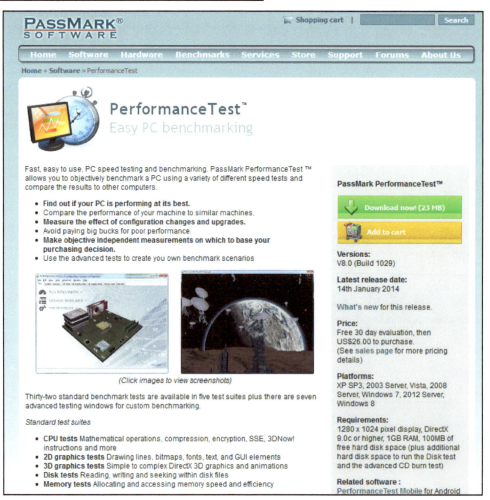

## CHECKING A TOWER POWER SUPPLY FOR 20 PIN ATX CONNECTOR

### Checking a Tower Power Supply¶

PURPOSE: This procedure is meant to verify that the Power Supply is providing the correct voltages:¶

- → +3.3 V¶
- → +/- 12V¶
- → +/- 5V¶
- → +5V Power Good Signal¶

MATERIALS: DPC Power Supply, Fluke DC Voltmeter, One Black Alligator-To-Alligator Jumper, Paper Clip, AC Power Input Cable, long nose pliers with wire cutter¶

PROCEDURE:¶

1. → Remove the power supply from the Tower.¶
2. → Open the power input switch on the rear of the power supply (0 down, 1 up)¶
3. → Make sure that the power cord in NOT connected.¶
4. → Cut and form a paper clip so as to fit into the pins on the 20 pin connector as shown below. (pins 14 green & pin 16 black)¶
5. → Instructor_____¶

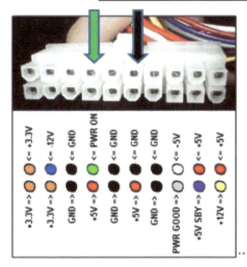 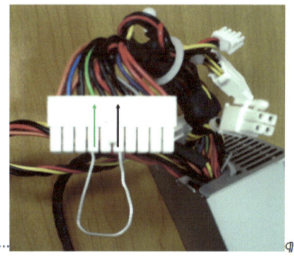

6. → Plug in the main power cord and close the switch on the rear.¶
7. → THE FAN SHOULD BEGIN RUNNING. IF not, the power supply is very likely bad. Turn off the switch immediately so that in the event that there is a short within the power supply, it will not have a chance to overheat.¶
8. → IF THE FAN RUNS, then use the Fluke meter to verify the output voltages as shown in the pin layout above. Do this by connecting the BLACK meter lead to the paperclip jumper. Use the RED to measure the voltages.¶

24 PIN ATX PIN LAYOUT & PINS TO BE JUMPERED

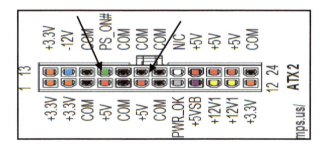

## BACKUP AND RESTORE WINDOWS XP USER FILES

**BACKING UP THE USER FILES**

1. Using your FLASH DISK as your backup device, insert it into any USB port.
2. Right-click the START BUTTON. Open the Windows Explorer. On the left side, under Documents and Settings, click on the folder for your account. The My Documents, Desktop, and Favorites folders (plus others) appear in the right pane.
3. In the right pane, using the CTRL key, select the MY DOCUMENTS, DESKTOP, AND FAVORITES folders so that they are all highlighted.
4. Right-click any one of the three, and click Properties. Write the SIZE as given in actual bytes (not the rounded off)
5. Right-click any one of the three, then SEND TO your flash disk.
6. On the flash disk, right click and make a new folder BACKUP MM/DD/YYYY. Drag each of the three backed-up folders into the new folder.
7. Check the Properties of the BACKUP folder and note the size in bytes. How does it compare with the size taken above?

**RESTORING THE USER FILES FOLLOWING A CLEAN INSTALL**

1. Install the flash disk. Using Windows Explorer, find your flash disk in the left pane and select it with one left click.
2. In the right pane, double-click the BACKUP folder so that each of the three backed-up folders appears.
3. One at a time, drag the folder from the right pane to the left pane placing it on top of the account folder (probably Student). This should merge the backed-up folder with the empty account folder.
4. Close out of the Explorer. From the START MENU, verify that the MY DOCUMENTS and MY PICTURES have all been restored.

## Using Synctoy for Incremental Backup

1. Using Firefox, download and install the 32 or 64 bit version of SYNCTOY from the Microsoft Download Center. NOTE: You might have to install the .net Framework 2.1 and the Microsoft Sync Framework 2.1 in order to make the install work.

2. Create folder pairs within SYNCTOY for DESKTOP to DESKTOP, for MY DOCUMENTS to MY DOCUMENTS, and PICTURES to PICTURES

3. Run Synctoy in ALL FOLDER PAIRS MODE. Check that the 3 folder pairs are equal to each other.

4. Randomly Add, Delete, Move, and Rename on both the left and right sides. Run Synctoy and verify that the left side and right side folders are equal.

## WINDOWS XP REPAIR

### Repairing Windows XP

**PURPOSE**: Repairing a Windows XP installation is valuable when you need to keep your programs and data intact but need to restore the Windows XP system files to their original state. This is often an easy fix for complicated Windows XP issues.

**PROCEDURE**:

1. Boot from the Windows XP Recovery CD as provided. Follow the prompts as indicated below:

2. **PRESS THE ENTER KEY TO SETUP WINDOWS XP** (Note: do NOT press the R for repair here!)

3. Press **F8 to ACCEPT THE USER LICENSE AGREEMENT**

4. **Select the Windows installation** to be repaired.

5. Press **R to REPAIR** the Windows installation

6. **Wait** for the current Windows installation **files to be deleted**

7. **Wait** for the Installation Files from the CD **to be installed**.

8. The Windows **XP repair begins** following a reboot (**blue screen**)

9. Follow the **prompts** until the Windows installation **complete**.

10. **Check** that all of the application programs and user files have **not been written over** but are as they were before.
    **Check** the **Device Manager** for having all drivers installed as before the repair.

## BURNING AN ISO FILE TO A BOOTABLE CD

### Burning An ISO File To A Bootable CD

**PURPOSE**: An ISO file is an image of a CD, DVD, or BD (high definition Blu-ray Disc). It is often referred to as a single file representation of an entire CD, DVD, or BD. The entire contents of the disc can be precisely duplicated in a single ISO file. You can think of it as a box that holds all the parts to something that needs to be built. Software such as Windows 7 that is purchased online is often delivered as a download in ISO format.

**MATERIALS**: A blank CD, Windows 7 computer

**PROCEDURE**:

1.  Insert a **blank CD** into the CD/DVD RW drive.
2.  **Right-click** the downloaded ISO file and click **BURN DISC IMAGE**

### Burn disc image

3.
4.  With the **WINDOWS DISC IMAGE BURNER** window open, select the appropriate DISC BURNER DRIVE and check the **VERIFY DISC AFTER BURNING** checkbox.
5.  Click **BURN**.

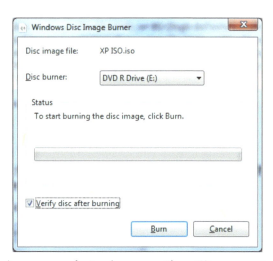

6.  Once the burning has completed, open the CD so as to view the files. Note that the files that were compacted in the ISO file have been separated into a bootable Windows XP installation CD.

## UPGRADING FROM WINDOWS XP TO WINDOWS 7

**UPGRADING FROM WINDOWS XP TO WINDOWS 7**

**PROCEDURE:**

1. Backup all user files.
2. From the Microsoft Download Center, download the Windows 7 Upgrade Advisor.
3. Install and run the Advisor checking for any issues that need to be addressed.
4. Perform installation of Windows 7:
   a. With Windows XP booted up and running, insert the Windows 7 DVD into the DVD drive
   b. Open MY Computer and double-click the DVD drive.
   c. Double-click the Setup.exe file to start the installation.
   d. Download Important Updates when suggested.
   e. Accept the license terms.
   f. Custom installation.
   g. Insert the Product Key
   h. Follow the prompts to completion of the install.
5. Check the Device Manager for any "yellow" missing drivers especially the LAN Network.
6. From the Start Menu, click Windows Updates and install critical updates.
7. Check the Windows Compatibility Center for links to drivers that have not yet been installed.
8. Restore user files.

## Using the USB IDE/SATA Drive Adapter

### Using the USB IDE/SATA Drive Adapter

<u>PURPOSE</u>: In the event of a hardware failure (motherboard) or software failure (virus or Windows corrupted) and there is a need to get the user files off of the hard drive and onto another computer, the Drive Adapter tool provides the means for transferring the files of concern.

<u>PROCEDURE</u>:

1.  Remove the hard drive and cable it to the IDE/SATA Drive Adapter.
2.  Apply power and cable it to any USB port on a working computer.
3.  Using Computer, locate and copy all of the user files to a flash disk.
4.  Copy the files from the flash disk to the new, working computer.

# Backup and Restore of Outlook Mail (pg. 1)

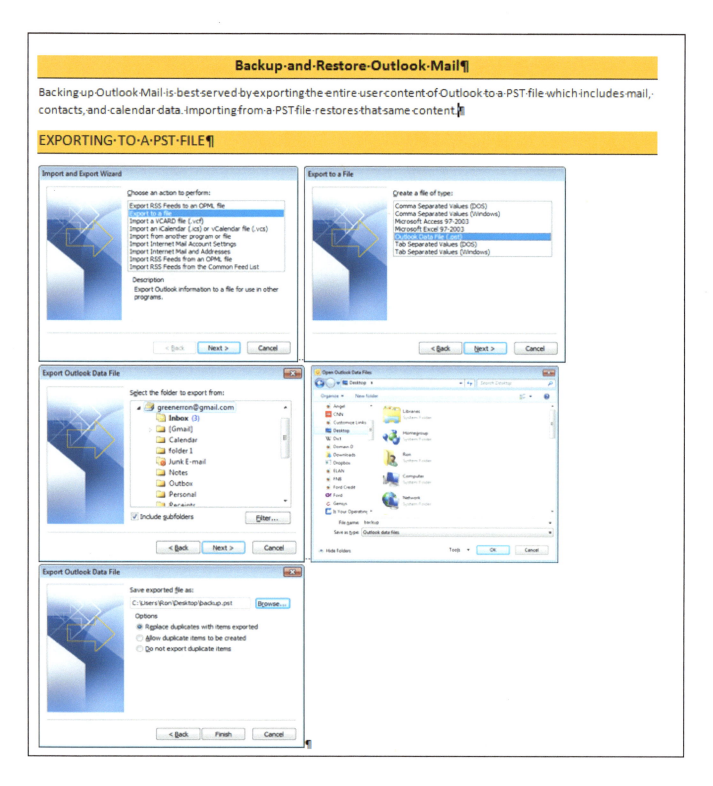

**Backup·and·Restore·Outlook·Mail¶**

Backing·up·Outlook·Mail·is·best·served·by·exporting·the·entire·user·content·of·Outlook·to·a·PST·file·which·includes·mail,· contacts,·and·calendar·data.·Importing·from·a·PST·file·restores·that·same·content.¶

## EXPORTING·TO·A·PST·FILE¶

# Backup and Restore of Outlook Mail (pg. 2)

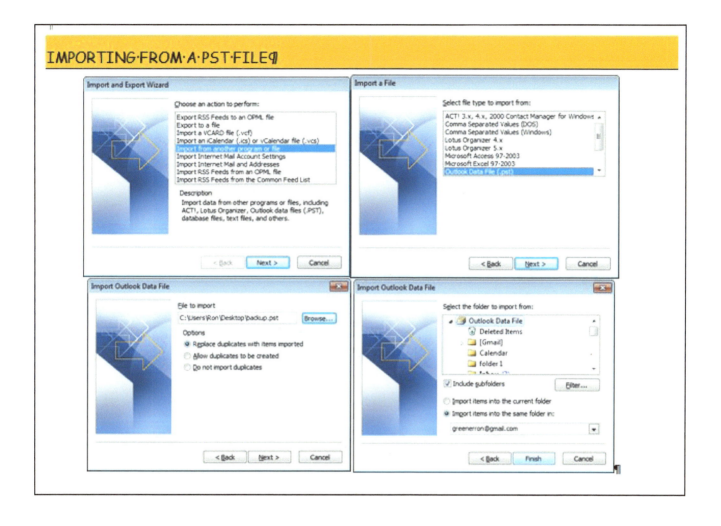

www.ingramcontent.com/pod-product-compliance
Lightning Source LLC
LaVergne TN
LVHW071523070326

832902LV00002B/61